THE LITTLE BOOK OF
JOE BIDEN

Published by OH!
20 Mortimer Street
London W1T 3JW

ISBN 978-1-80069-131-5

Compiled by: Lisa Dyer
Editorial: Theresa Bebbington
Project manager: Russell Porter
Design: Andy Jones
Production: Freencky Portas

A CIP catalogue record for this book is available from the British Library

Printed in Dubai

10 9 8 7 6 5 4 3 2 1

Cover image: (Digital composite) © Pete Marovich/Getty Images
& Tasos Katopodis/Getty Images

THE LITTLE BOOK OF

JOE BIDEN

QUOTES TO LIVE BY

CONTENTS

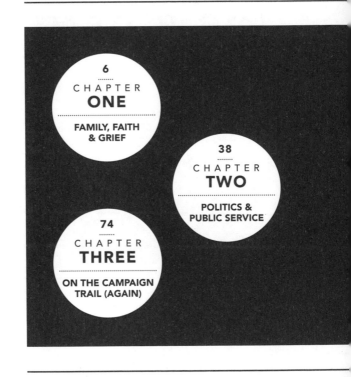

CHAPTER
ONE

FAMILY, FAITH & GRIEF

From a debilitating stutter and a
humble upbringing to the tragic loss
of his first wife and baby daughter,
and later his son Beau, Joe Biden's
life story has given him a unique
ability to connect with the
average person.

[My mother] taught us never to be intimated by power, wealth, or station . . . We could set our own standard, one that was based on character alone.

Funeral service for his mother, "Jean" Finnegan Biden, January 12, 2010

You know, folks, my dad used to have an expression. He'd say, 'A father knows he's a success when he turns and looks at his son or daughter and knows that they turned out better than he did.'

Democratic National Convention, August 27, 2008

I used to stutter really badly. Everybody thinks it's funny. And it's not funny. It's not . . . You never make fun of anybody with a club foot or a withered arm, but it's open season on anybody who stutters.

Archmere Academy speech, May 17, 2013

I learned so much from having to deal with stuttering. It gave me insight into other people's pain, other people's suffering.

American Institute for Stuttering speech, June 17, 2016

The one thing I want my kids to remember about me is that I was an athlete. The hell with the rest of this stuff.

People *magazine, August 25, 2008*

From this house to the
White House with the grace
of God.

*Message he wrote on one of the walls of his childhood
home in Scranton, Pennsylvania, on the morning of the
presidential election, November 3, 2020*

There's no such thing as quality time. Every important thing your child will say to you will be off script . . . will be at a time when you don't expect it.

Tonight Show with Jimmy Fallon, *September 29, 2016*

I began to commute . . . from Washington to Wilmington, which I've done for over 37 years. I did it because I wanted to be able to kiss them goodnight and kiss them in the morning the next day . . . But looking back on it, the truth be told, the real reason I went home every night was that I needed my children more than they needed me.

Yale University Class Day speech, May 17, 2015

"

I learned early on what I wanted to do, what fulfilled me the most, what made me happy— my family, my faith, and being engaged in the public affairs that gripped my generation.

"

Yale University Class Day speech,
May 17, 2015

My own father had always said the measure of a man wasn't how many times or how hard he got knocked down, but how fast he got back up.

Promises to Keep *(2008)*

66

My dad used to say, 'the greatest sin of all is the abuse of power, and the cardinal sin of all, is a man raising his hand or taking advantage of a woman.'

99

Late Night with Seth Meyers,
October 2016

My dad would say, 'Joe, remember, never argue with your wife about anything that is going to happen more than a year from now.'

Esquire *magazine, December 14, 2011*

I'd rather be at home making love to my wife while my children are asleep.

When discussing whether he would run for president, June 22, 2006

I've been sleeping with a teacher for a long time. But it's always been the same teacher.

National Teacher of the Year reception, April 26, 2010

As a child of God, I believe my rights are not derived from the Constitution . . . My rights are because I exist. They were given to me and each of my fellow citizens by our Creator.

Promises to Keep *(2008)*

I have the great advantage of my faith, the Catholic social doctrine, and my political views coincide . . . You are your brother's keeper.

Facebook, November 3, 2020

For so many in our nation, this is a dark, dark time. So where do we turn? Faith. Faith provides clarity and solace.

National Prayer Breakfast,
February 4, 2021

And all the good things that have happened, have happened around the culture of my religion and the theology of my religion.

The Late Show with Stephen Colbert, *September 11, 2015*

I felt trapped in a constant twilight of vertigo, like in the dream where you're suddenly falling, only I was constantly falling . . . But I'd look at Beau and Hunter asleep . . . And I knew I had no choice but to fight to stay alive.

About the death of his first wife, Neila, and daughter, Promises to Keep *(2008)*

Most guys don't really know what I lost, because they never knew what I had . . . When you lose something like that, you lose a part of yourself that you never get back again.

About the death of his first wife,
Washingtonian, *1974*

I began to understand how despair led people to just cash it in; how suicide wasn't just an option but a rational option.

On grief, Promises to Keep *(2008)*

66

But by focusing on my sons,
I found my redemption . . .
The incredible bond I have with
my children is the gift I'm not
sure I would have had, had
I not been through what I
went through.

99

Yale University Class Day speech, May 17, 2015

―――――――――――――――――――――

"

I felt God had played a horrible trick on me, and I was angry. I found no comfort in the Church. So I kept walking the dark streets to try to exhaust the rage.

"

Promises to Keep *(2008)*

―――――――――――――――――――――

For the first time in my life, I understood how someone could consciously decide to commit suicide. Not because they were deranged, not because they were nuts, because they had been to the top of the mountain, and they just knew in their heart they would never get there again.

Tragedy Assistance Program for Survivors (TAPS) Seminar, May 25, 2012

The only way I survived, the only way I got through it, was by staying busy and keeping my mind, when it can be, focused on my job.

On son Beau's death, Promise Me, Dad *(2017)*

The greatest gift is the ability to forget—to forget the bad things and focus on the good.

Detroit, Michigan, January 16, 2014

But you know you are going to make it when the image of your dad, your husband, your friend crosses your mind and a smile comes to your lips before a tear to your eye.

Eulogy for John McCain, Arizona, August 30, 2018

What does it really cost to take a moment to look someone in the eye, to give him a hug, to let her know, I get it. You're not alone?

Promise Me, Dad *(2017)*

Funerals are for the living, I have always believed, and the job of the eulogist is to acknowledge the enormity of the loss they have just suffered and to help them appreciate that the legacy and accomplishments of their loved one have not died with them.

Promise Me, Dad *(2017)*

Because there's so many funerals I've attended, so many bases I've visited. And you know, not all losses are equal. Not all losses are equal.

Tragedy Assistance Program for Survivors (TAPS) Seminar, May 25, 2012

CHAPTER
TWO

POLITICS & PUBLIC SERVICE

Known for forging partnerships across the aisle in the Senate, Joe has also had his fair share of hopping from side to side on issues such as crime, guns, and drugs. But his optimism, compassion, and sense of fair play have never wavered.

Hell, I might be president now if it weren't for the fact I said I had an uncle who was a coal miner. Turns out I didn't have anybody in the coal mines, you know what I mean?

The Daily Show with Jon Stewart, *July 28, 2004*

I can die a happy man never having been President of the United States of America. But it doesn't mean I won't run.

99

GQ *magazine, July 18, 2013*

I never had an interest in being a mayor 'cause that's a real job. You have to produce. That's why I was able to be a senator for 36 years.

At a Democratic fund raiser in Chicago, Washington Examiner, *March 30, 2012*

Except for 'father,' there is no other title, including 'Vice President', that I am more proud to wear than 'Senator.'

On resigning his Senate seat to become vice president, January 21, 2009

My mother believed and my father believed that if I wanted to be President of the United States, I could be, I could be . . . Vice President!

Youngstown, Ohio, May 16, 2012

There is no inherent power in the office of the vice presidency. Zero. None. It's all a reflection of your relationship with the president.

The Late Show with Stephen Colbert, *September 11, 2015*

Remember, no one decides who they're going to vote for based on the vice president. I mean that literally.

99

The New York Times, *September 19, 2008*

Isn't it a bitch? This vice president thing? . . . That was a joke, that was a joke. Best decision I ever made. I'm joking. That was a joke.

To the student-body vice president, Harvard University, October 2, 2014

You're president, if you conclude my judgment is not the right judgment, I abide by that, but I want an opportunity to have an input.

To President Obama, as told on Larry King Live, *December 22, 2008*

"

In my heart I'm confident I would make a good president.

"

The Today Show, *NBC, January 29, 2014*

I remain captivated by
the possibilities of politics
and public service. In fact, I
believe—as I know my grandpop
did—that my chosen profession
is a noble calling.

Promises to Keep *(2008)*

Part of being a public servant, I came to understand in 1978, was absorbing the anger of people who don't know where to turn. If I couldn't solve the problem for them, I had to at least be an outlet.

Promises to Keep *(2008)*

66

I have never left another senator out to dry. Never.

99

The New Yorker, *October 13, 2008*

If you're ever working with me and I hear you treating another colleague with disrespect, talking down to someone, I will fire you on the spot.

Swearing-in ceremony, January 20, 2020

I read in *The New York Times* today that one of my problems if I were to run for president [is that] I like Republicans. OK, well, bless me Father for I have sinned.

CNN, January 24, 2019

You've got to reach a hand
of friendship across the aisle
and across philosophies in
this country.

Everyday Power, October 28, 2020

It's time to unite America, and we'll do that by choosing hope over fear, science over fiction, truth over lies, and unity over division. Democracy requires consensus.

99

Ohio campaign rally, October 13, 2020

Politics doesn't have to be a raging fire, destroying everything in its path. Every disagreement doesn't have to be a cause for total war. And we must reject the culture in which facts themselves are manipulated, and even manufactured.

Inaugural Address, January 20, 2021

Politics was a matter of personal honor. A man's word is his bond. You give your word, you keep it. **99**

Promises to Keep *(2008)*

Leadership, at its core, in my view, is about being personal . . . You always put yourself in the other person's position, and then also to understand where they're coming from, whether it's a major foreign leader or a friend.

Interview with Brené Brown, October 21, 2020

My message to everyone struggling right now is this: Help is on the way.

Twitter, December 1, 2020

Don't tell me what you value.
Show me your budget, and I'll
tell you what you value.

"

St. Clair Shores, Michigan, September 15, 2008

In the twenty-first century, the countries that thrive will be the ones where citizens know their voices will be heard, because the institutions are transparent.

Romanian Civil Society Groups and Students speech, May 21, 2014

It's important to read the reports and listen to the experts, [but] more important is being able to read people in power.

Promises to Keep *(2008)*

If you have a piece of crack cocaine no bigger than this quarter that I am holding in my hand . . . we passed a law that said you go to jail for five years. You get no probation. You get nothing other than five years in jail. Judge doesn't have a choice.

On a crime bill he crafted with segregationist Strom Thurmond, June 20,1991

66
We do everything but hang people for jaywalking in this bill.
99

Tough on crime in the Senate, May 14, 1992

And let me tell you something, folks, people are driving across that border with tons, tons, hear me, tons of everything from byproducts for methamphetamine to cocaine to heroin and it's all coming up through corrupt Mexico.

Arguing for a Wall, South Carolina Rotary Club, November 27, 2006

I didn't argue that the war in Vietnam was immoral; it was merely stupid and a horrendous waste of time, money, and lives based on a flawed premise.

Promises to Keep *(2008)*

If you need more than ten
rounds to hunt . . . you shouldn't
be hunting. If you can't get
the deer in three shots, you
shouldn't be hunting. You
are an embarrassment.

99

National Public Radio, March 20, 2013

Use a shotgun on someone
invading your home and you
don't kill your kids—use an
AR-15, it goes through your
wall and it can kill your kid in
the bedroom.

Insider, *April 13, 2013*

66

I'm a liberal on health care because I believe it is a birth right of every human being— not just some damn privilege to be meted out to a few people. But when it comes to issues like abortion, amnesty, and acid, I'm about as liberal as your grandmother.

99

"Death and the All-American Boy" by Kitty Kelly,
Washingtonian, 1974

I am absolutely comfortable with the fact that men marrying men, women marrying women, and heterosexual men and women marrying another are entitled to the same exact rights.

Meet the Press, *May 6, 2012*

I wasn't built to look the other way because the law demanded it. The law might be wrong.

Promises to Keep *(2008)*

Fighting corruption is not just good governance. It's self-defense. It's patriotism.

Global Entrepreneurship Summit speech, November 20, 2014

CHAPTER
THREE

ON THE CAMPAIGN TRAIL (AGAIN)

Joe may have spent many years on the campaign trail, but he's not immune from making the occasional rookie error. Knocked down, he got up again and again, making it third time lucky for president on his 2020 run.

In this world, emotion has become suspect—the accepted style is smooth, antiseptic, and passionless.

Announcing his run for the presidency, June 9, 1987

I'm not exploring. I'm in.
And this is the beginning
of a marathon.

Announcing his run for the presidency, January 30, 2007

The core values of this nation, our standing in the world, our very democracy, everything that has made America, is at stake. That's why today I'm announcing my candidacy for President of the United States.

Announcing his run for the presidency, April 25, 2019

We're in a battle for the soul of
this nation. Who we are, what
we stand for, and who we want
to be—it's all at stake.

Gettysburg, Pennsylvania, October 6, 2020

People ask if I can compete with the money of Hillary and Barack. I hope at the end of the day, they can compete with my ideas and my experience.

NBC, January 31, 2007

There's only three things he mentions in a sentence: a noun, a verb, and 9/11.

About Rudy Giuliani, Democratic primary debate, October 30, 2007

An opportunity missed is not the same as an opportunity lost. Not yet.

On the campaign trail in Iowa, October 2008

I have been able to reach across the aisle. I think it's fair to say that I have almost as many friends on the Republican side of the aisle as I do the Democratic side of the aisle.

Vice-presidential debate, October 2, 2008

[Hillary] is as qualified or more qualified than I am to be Vice President of the United States. . . . Quite frankly, it might have been a better pick than me.

An endorsement of Hillary Clinton during a campaign rally, September 10, 2008

"

I could hear people murmuring under their breath: 'There he is . . . Goddam Biden . . . Kill the sonofabitch.' And these were my voters—working-class Democrats.

"

Promises to Keep *(2008)*

When sea gull droppings landed on my head at a campaign event at Bowers Beach two days before Election Day, I chose to read it as a sign of a coming success.

Promises to Keep *(2008)*

This guy doesn't have a clue about the middle class. Not a clue . . . He has no clue about what makes America great. Actually, he has no clue. Period.

About Donald Trump, Democratic National Convention, July 27, 2016

And you wanna check my shape, let's do push-ups together, man. Let's run, let's do whatever you wanna do. Let's take an IQ test.

An attendee questions whether Biden's age should be a factor in voting for him, Iowa town hall, December 5, 2019

You ever been to a caucus? No, you haven't. You're a lying dog-faced pony soldier.

A voter questions Biden's poor performance in the Iowa caucuses, February 9, 2020

Will you shut up, man? . . . It's hard to get any word in with this clown.

To President Donald Trump, at the presidential debate, September 30, 2020

You're a damn liar, man. That's not true, and no one has ever said that. You see it on the TV, I know you do.

To a voter who accused Biden of getting his son a job at the Ukrainian gas company Burisma, Iowa town hall, December 5, 2019

You ought to go vote for someone else.

To voter Ed Fallon, who lobbied Biden to denounce a proposed gas pipeline, January 28, 2020

You've got one job here, keep the guys away from your sister.

To the brothers of a thirteen year old, on the campaign trail, Iowa, 2019

66

With all due respect, that's
a bunch of malarkey.

99

*To then-House Speaker Paul Ryan at the vice-presidential
debate, October 11, 2012*

What's he do? He just pours gasoline on the fire constantly.

*About Donald Trump, presidential debate,
September 30, 2020*

CHAPTER
FOUR

FOLKSY
WORDS &
WISDOM

Homespun, caring, and empathetic,
if also long-winded and rambling,
"Uncle Joe" frequently dispenses
heartfelt advice, family anecdotes,
and aphorisms, sprinkled with quaint
Bidenisms, such as "bunch of
malarkey" and "God love ya."

True bravery is when there is
very little chance of winning,
but you keep fighting.

Promise Me, Dad *(2017)*

Fear never builds the future, but hope does.

Instagram, December 2, 2020

We Irish are the only people in the world who are actually nostalgic about the future.

Promise Me, Dad *(2017)*

Failure at some point in your life is inevitable, but giving up is unforgivable.

Democratic National Convention, August 27, 2008

There's no accounting for what fate will deal you. There are some days when we need a hand. There are other days when we are called on to lend one.

Inaugural Address, January 20, 2021

When I listen to some of the stuff Donald Trump says, it just makes me sad. It's never, never been wise to try and appeal to the darker side of human nature.

Billboard, *March 30, 2016*

A job is about a lot more than a paycheck. It's about dignity, it's about respect, it's about being able to look your kid in the eye and say everything is going to be OK.

Twitter, October 25, 2019

As my mom would say, 'Joey, as long as a person's alive, they have the obligation to strive. They're not dead until they've seen the face of God.'

Esquire *magazine, December 14, 2011*

Remember, no serious guys until you're 30.

Questionable advice to young women, as quoted in The New Yorker, July 28, 2014

I know I'm not supposed to like muscle cars, but I like muscle cars.

At a Ford automobile plant in Michigan,
The New York Times, *September 19, 2008*

Violence against women is a stain on the moral character of a society, in any society in which it occurs.

International Human Rights Day, December 10, 2014

Treating people with dignity and respect should be the baseline for how we act to one another.

Facebook, November 3, 2020

My dad used to have an expression: 'It is the lucky person who gets up in the morning, puts both feet on the floor, knows what they are about to do, and thinks it still matters.'

Yale University Class Day, May 17, 2015

Just because our political heroes were murdered does not mean that the dream does not still live, buried deep in our broken hearts.

Promises to Keep *(2008)*

The only thing I know is I ain't changing my brand. I know what I believe. I'm confident in what I know. And I'm gonna say it. And if folks like it, wonderful. If they don't like it, I understand.

Politico *magazine, March/April 2014*

I was raised by a tough, compassionate Irish lady named Catherine Eugenia Finnegan Biden. And she taught all of her children that, but for the grace of God, there go you.

Yale University Class Day speech, May 17, 2015

There's an old Irish proverb that some of you know that I heard my grandfather use but never really apply to me before. He said, 'a silent mouth is sweet to hear.'

Introducing President Barack Obama, Washington, D.C., March 17, 2010

My dad used to say, 'Joey, I don't expect the government to solve my problems. But I expect it to understand my problems.'

Twitter, December 5, 2020

66

Life is a matter of really tough
choices.

99

Meet the Press, *December 19, 2010*

Reality has a way of intruding.
Reality eventually intrudes on
everything.

GQ magazine, July 18, 2013

My dad had an expression:
'Joey, don't compare me
to the Almighty, compare
me to the alternative.'

The Washington Post, *January 25, 2020*

I exaggerate when I'm angry, but I've never gone around telling people things that aren't true about me.

The New York Times, *September 21, 1987*

I won't traffic in fear and division. I won't fan the flames of hate. I will seek to heal the racial wounds that have long plagued this country—not use them for political gain.

Philadelphia, May 29, 2020

No one can tell me that if it had been a group of Black Lives Matter protestors yesterday that they wouldn't have been treated very differently than the mob that stormed the Capitol. We all know that's true—and it's unacceptable.

Twitter, January 7, 2021

Silence is complicity. Silence is consent.

About Harvey Weinstein and the #MeToo movement, NBC, October 12, 2017

We must stand up and demand that we no longer give this hate safe harbor; that homophobia and racism have no place on our streets or in our hearts.

Twitter, January 29, 2019

CHAPTER
FIVE

OFF SCRIPT

Biden's many gaffes, slipups, faux pas, and foot in mouths throughout his 50-year career are legendary. Often attributed to his lifelong struggle with his stutter or his no-filter plain speaking, they can be hilarious . . . or deeply offensive.

Folks, I can tell you I've known eight presidents, three of them intimately.

Campaign event in Detroit, Michigan, August 22, 2012

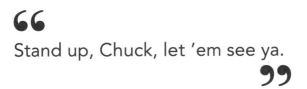

Stand up, Chuck, let 'em see ya.

To Missouri State Senator Chuck Graham,
while he was in a wheelchair, September 12, 2008

When the stock market crashed, Franklin Roosevelt got on the television and he didn't just talk about the princes of greed. He said, 'Look, here's what happened.'

In the Great Crash of 1929, Herbert Hoover was president and TVs weren't yet manufactured. CBS, September 22, 2008

A man I'm proud to call my friend. A man who will be the next President of the United States: Barack America!

At his first campaign rally with Barack Obama, August 23, 2008

You cannot go to a 7-11 or a Dunkin' Donuts unless you have a slight Indian accent . . . I'm not joking.

99

In a private remark to an Indian-American man caught on C-SPAN, June 2006

. . . to assure a certain number of Blacks, Chicanos, or whatever in each school. That, to me, is the most racist concept you can come up with.

On busing, The Washington Post, *October 2, 1975*

[Mitt Romney] said in the first 100 days, he's going to let the big banks write their own rules—unchain Wall Street. They're going to put y'all back in chains.

Speaking to a largely African-American audience, August 14, 2012

It doesn't matter whether or not they are the victims of society. The end result is they are about to knock my mother on the head with a lead pipe, shoot my sister, beat up my wife, take on my sons.

99

On a crime bill concerning "predators on our streets" in the Senate, November 1993

I mean, we may not want to demonize anybody who has made money . . . No one's standard of living will change, nothing would fundamentally change.

Speaking to wealthy donors in New York, June 18, 2019

I mean, you got the first mainstream African-American who is articulate and bright and clean and a nice-looking guy. I mean, that's a storybook, man.

Of Barack Obama, The New York Observer, *February 1, 2007*

"

His mom lived in Long Island for ten years or so, God rest her soul. Although she's, wait . . . Your mom's still alive. It was your dad that passed. God bless her soul. I gotta get this straight.

"

Biden mistakenly gave Irish Prime Minister Brian Cowen his condolences for losing the wrong parent, St. Patrick's Day reception, 2010

We hold these truths to be self-
evident. All men and women are
created, by the, you know, you
know, the thing.

Biden botches the Declaration of Independence,
Washington Examiner, *March 2, 2020*

Poor kids are just as bright
and just as talented as white
kids.

The New York Times, *August 9, 2019*

Corn Pop was a bad dude, and he ran a bunch of bad boys . . . He was waiting for me with three guys with straight razors. Not a joke.

Biden claims he personally fended off a gang leader, June 26, 2017

Unless we do something about this, my children are going to grow up in a jungle, the jungle being a racial jungle . . .

99

On busing, during a Congressional session, July 1977

We have to hold every drug user accountable, because if there are no drug users, there'd be no appetite for drugs.

On blaming drug users instead of dealers, September 5, 1989

Understand that in Washington, D.C., a gaffe is when you tell the truth.

National Association of Black Journalists, June 21, 2012

I promise you—the president has a big stick. I promise you.

About Barack Obama, New York University, April 26, 2012

"

During the '60s, I was in fact very concerned about the civil rights movement. I was not an activist. I worked at an all-Black swimming pool in the east side of Wilmington, Delaware. I was involved. I was involved in what they were thinking, what they were feeling. I was involved, but I was not out marching.

"

News conference, September 17, 1987

66

We've got to recognize that a kid wearing a hoodie may very well be the next poet laureate— not a gangbanger.

99

Speaking at the Rainbow PUSH Coalition, June 28, 2019

We have to take care of the cure. That will make the problem worse, no matter what.

Talking about the COVID-19 pandemic, on The View, *March 2020*

And, by the way, the 20, the 200 mil—the 200,000 people that have died on [Trump's] watch, how many of those have survived?

Biden-Trump presidential debate, September 29, 2020

> **"**
> I will develop some disease and say I have to resign.
> **"**

When asked what he would do to solve a serious disagreement with Vice President Harris, CNN, December 4, 2020

Clap for that, you stupid bastards.

Remarking on the lackluster response to his speech to the 380th Air Expeditionary Wing stationed in Abu Dhabi, 2016

The younger generation now tells me how tough things are. Give me a break!

Los Angeles Times, *January 11, 2018*

So I learned about roaches and I learned about kids jumping on my lap. And I loved kids jumping on my lap.

Discussing his experience working at a pool in his youth, December 1, 2019

Well, I tell you what, if you have a problem figuring out whether you're for me or Trump, then you ain't Black. Take a look at my record, man!

Disastrous remark on radio host Charlamagne tha God's Breakfast Club show, May 22, 2020

I spent last summer going through the Black sections of my town, holding rallies in parks, trying to get Black men to understand it is not unmanly to wear a condom, getting women to understand they can say no, getting people in the position where testing matters. I got tested for AIDS. I know Barack got tested for AIDS.

Howard University, June 28, 2007

I'm not sorry for any of my intentions. I'm not sorry for anything that I have ever done. I have never been disrespectful intentionally to a man or a woman. So that's not the reputation that I've had since high school, for God's sake.

As quoted in The Hill, *April 5, 2019*

If we do everything right, if we do it with absolute certainty, there's still a 30 percent chance we're going to get it wrong.

Adding up the percentages. On the stimulus bill, February 6, 2009

What I'm trying to say without boring you too long at breakfast, and you all look dull as hell, I might add. The dullest audience I have ever spoken to. Just sitting there, staring at me. Pretend you like me!

To Turkish-American and Azerbaijani-American donors, April 27, 2012

I wouldn't go anywhere in confined places now. When one person sneezes, it goes all the way through the aircraft.

On swine flu, The Today Show, *NBC, April 30, 2009*

I ain't dead and I'm not gonna die. #Joementum.

Twitter, March 4, 2020

I probably shouldn't say this,
but then again I'm Joe Biden.
No one ever doubts that I mean
what I say. The problem is I
sometimes say all that I mean.

National Governors Association, June 11, 2014

I am a gaffe machine. But, my God, what a wonderful thing compared to a guy who can't tell the truth.

CNN, December 4, 2018

You know, I'm embarrassed. Do you know the website number? I should have it in front of me and I don't.

On the link to a government site, Early Show, *CBS, February 25, 2009*

This is a big f**king deal!

Caught congratulating President Barack Obama during the health-care signing ceremony, Washington, D.C., March 23, 2010

Here I am, the first Irish Catholic vice president in the history of United States of America. Barack Obama is the first African-American in the history of the United States of America.

Forgetting the key word "president," at the Radio and Television Correspondents' Dinner, Washington, D.C., March 17, 2010

Look, John [McCain's] last-minute economic plan does nothing to tackle the No. 1 job facing the middle class, and it happens to be, as Barack says, a three-letter word: jobs. J-O-B-S, jobs.

October 15, 2008

I said that if we were in high school, I'd take him out behind the gym and beat the hell out of him.

About Donald Trump, in reference to the Access Hollywood tape, March 21, 2018

I know I'm called Middle-class Joe. It's not meant as a compliment, I'm not sophisticated.

Congressional rally in Kentucky, October 12, 2018

That's why I've made it a priority my entire career to work closely with you, from the time I got to the Senate, 180 years ago.

Joking at the U.S. Conference of Mayors, September 26, 2020

CHAPTER
SIX

AMERICA, HOME & ABROAD

When it comes to love for, and belief in, his country, Joe is at his most eloquent and inspiring, passionately endorsing American values and democracy to the nation and the world at large.

Finding light in the darkness
is a very American thing to
do. In fact, it may be the most
American thing we do.

Twitter, March 11, 2021

But I need you, the American
people. I need you.

Speech at the one-year anniversary of the pandemic,
March 11, 2021

America is an idea. An idea that is stronger than any army, bigger than any ocean, more powerful than any dictator or tyrant. It gives hope to the most desperate people on earth, it guarantees that everyone is treated with dignity and gives hate no safe harbor.

Announcing his run for the presidency, April 25, 2019

The twenty-first century is going to be the American century. Because we lead not only by the example of our power, but by the power of our example.

Democratic National Convention,
July 27, 2016

Our future cannot depend on the government alone. The ultimate solutions lie in the attitudes and the actions of the American people.

The New York Times, *June 10, 1987*

No fundamental social
change occurs merely because
government acts. It's because
civil society, the conscience
of a country, begins to rise
up and demand, demand,
demand change.

Remarks to the press in Guatemala, June 20, 2014

For too long in this society, we have celebrated unrestrained individualism over common community.

Announcing running in the U.S. presidential race, June 9, 1987

America cannot retreat from the world. We cannot succumb to the isolationist instincts of those who would put up trade walls to keep out the world . . .

Announcing running in the U.S. presidential race,
June 9, 1987

We didn't crumble after 9/11. We didn't falter after the Boston Marathon. But we're America. Americans will never, ever stand down. We endure. We overcome. We own the finish line.

Harvard University's Kennedy School,
October 2, 2014

Given a fair shot, given a
fair chance, Americans have
never, ever, ever, ever let their
country down. Never. Never.
Ordinary people like us. Who do
extraordinary things.

Democratic National Convention,
July 27, 2016

Wall Street didn't build this country—the middle class did. And unions built the middle class.

Twitter, September 7, 2020

Look folks, we know who built this country and we know who is going to rebuild it. It's you. Instead of vilifying you, we should be thanking you. We owe you!

Hardball with Chris Matthews, *NBC, September 6, 2012*

The American public's a lot
more sophisticated than we all
give them credit for. And on
complicated issues, I'm going
to give them straight answers.
And if it takes more than three
minutes, I'm going to do it.

Good Morning America, *ABC, January 31, 2007*

Let me tell you what I literally told every world leader I've met with, and I've met them all: It's never, never, never been a good bet to bet against America. We have the finest fighting force in the world.

Democratic National Convention,
July 27, 2016

Democracy doesn't happen by accident. We have to defend it, fight for it, strengthen it, renew it.

Munich Security Conference, February 19, 2021

We Americans think, in every
country in transition, there's a
Thomas Jefferson hiding behind
some rock or a James Madison
beyond one sand dune.

Harvard University's Kennedy School,
October 2, 2014

You want to know whether we're better off? I've got a little bumper sticker for you: Osama bin Laden is dead and General Motors is alive!

Labor Day Rally, September 3, 2012

To make progress, we have to stop treating our opponents as enemies. We are not enemies. What brings us together as Americans is so much stronger than anything that can tear us apart.

Public address, as the 2020 presidential vote count continued, November 4, 2020

Our nation is shaped by the constant battle between our better angels and our darkest impulses. It is time for our better angels to prevail.

Victory speech as U.S. President-elect, November 7, 2020

Love is more powerful than hate.
Hope is more powerful than fear.
Light is more powerful dark.
This is our moment. This is
our mission.

Twitter, August 22, 2020

We must end this uncivil war that pits red against blue, rural versus urban, conservative versus liberal. We can do this, if we open our souls instead of hardening our hearts.

Inaugural Address, January 20, 2021

The scenes of chaos at the Capitol do not reflect a true America. Do not represent who we are . . . This is not dissent. It's disorder. It's chaos. It borders on sedition. And it must end now.

CNN, January 6, 2021

The words of a president matter, no matter how good or bad that president is. At their best, the words of a president can inspire. At their worst, they can incite.

CNN, January 6, 2021